the complete

HALOGEN
OVEN COOKBOOK UK

EVERYDAY HALOGEN AIR FRYER COOKER RECIPES

 **CookNation**

BELL & MACKENZIE
PUBLISHING LIMITED

CONTENTS

The halogen oven is a remarkable appliance providing a space-saving, economical and affordable way to cook for your family. As well as cooking food beautifully, it can save time compared to a conventional oven (sometimes up to 40% quicker) and there's much less washing-up. It is the perfect all-rounder, delivering delicious meals in super-quick time, making it the go-to device for both busy people and the energy conscious.

What is a Halogen Oven?

You may already have a halogen oven or perhaps are contemplating buying one. Either way, a brief explanation of this remarkable appliance is worth a little time.

A halogen oven is an electrical worktop appliance which performs the same functions as a traditional oven, but can be operated at a fraction of the running cost and results in reduced cooking times.

This is possible because it uses a powerful halogen bulb housed in the lid of the unit to produce radiant infrared heat which, when circulated around the glass bowl of the appliance using convection currents driven by a powerful fan, cooks the food evenly and nearly twice as fast than a traditional fan assisted/gas oven. In addition, halogen ovens don't need to be pre-heated, except for some baking recipes.

Halogen ovens should not be confused with microwave ovens, which use radio waves to penetrate food, causing friction between water and fat molecules. This friction provides heat, which in turn cooks the food. Microwave cooking, while fast, often ends with poor results, such as cold spots within the dish or soggy bottoms! By contrast, when using a halogen oven, your food is cooked evenly, keeping it tender on the inside but can also be browned and crispy on the outside.

Typically, a halogen oven can reduce cooking times compared to a conventional oven by 20-30% and sometimes by up to 40%. This is made possible by the lower temperatures used and the reduced cooking time compared to a conventional oven. It is therefore perfect for bringing down costs associated with cooking and is a very energy efficient device. It's also a great way to cook healthier meals, as fat is drained away through the cooking racks.

Every unit will normally come with a low and high grill rack, tongs, a rack to place the lid of the appliance when adding/removing food (it becomes very hot) and sometimes an extender ring to increase the capacity of the oven (these can also be purchased separately). Some models come with a hinged lid, which means there is no need to completely remove the lid. This feature can be much safer, however, always be aware that the halogen element is VERY hot and should not be touched or placed on any surface that could get burned (use oven gloves when lifting the lid).

Always read the manufacturer's instructions prior to use. For advice on which model best suits your needs, refer to the Which Halogen Oven? section.

What are the benefits of cooking with a Halogen Oven?

Cooking times can be reduced by up to 40% compared to a conventional oven but there are many other advantages to cooking halogen-style:

Affordable. Depending which model you choose (more on that later!), prices range between £40-£70. This is a fraction of the cost of a conventional oven and cheaper than the popular air fryer method of cooking.

Economical. As well as the affordable price, halogen ovens are less expensive to run than a conventional oven. They are smaller, provide a constant temperature due to the circulation of air combined with the intense heat of the bulb, and use accurate temperature sensors. This means food cooks in less time, which in turn means less electricity and less cost. In addition, they heat up very quickly so lengthy pre-heating is generally not needed.

Multifunctional. Halogen ovens have many uses: they can roast, grill, bake, steam and defrost. Some models also allow cooking from frozen.

Healthy. Halogen ovens work best by circulating heat around the food. The use of the wire racks provided with the unit mean that if you are looking for a healthier way to cook your food, any excess fat produced while cooking drains away. Also, cooking with a halogen oven requires less additional oil and fats than a conventional oven.

Clarity. One of the great advantages of a halogen oven is that you can literally see your food cooking! The large glass bowl enables you to check on your food without opening the appliance, as you would with a conventional oven.

Self-cleaning. Although you can remove the glass bowl, most halogen ovens will come with a self-cleaning function. This is a pre-programmed function to clean your bowl using water and washing-up liquid.

Is there anything my Halogen Oven can't do?

Due to their size, there are limitations on the quantity of food you can cook. If you have a dinner party of 10 then perhaps the help of a conventional oven would be advised. Most appliances will comfortably cater for 4 people, although an extender ring may allow you to cook for more. For the purposes of this book, recipes serve a combination of 2 and 4, making it easier to either halve or double your quantities if needed.

Halogen ovens work best by circulating air around the food, so if too much is packed into the bowl or food is not placed on the racks, cooking times will increase. Similarly, heavily liquid-based dishes, such as soups, will require longer cooking times than you might expect. Vegetables, particularly root vegetables, can take longer than meat to cook in a halogen oven so they should be cut into smaller bitesize pieces. Pasta and rice should generally be pre-cooked. Use tinned pulses and beans rather than dried.

All of the above have been taken into consideration and addressed in our recipes.

Which Halogen Oven?

As with any new purchase, you should consider how you will use your appliance and, of course, the budget you can afford. If you are buying a halogen oven for the first time or replacing a model, we strongly recommend you spend some time researching customer reviews before parting with your money. There are several websites dedicated to halogen ovens that provide very useful comparisons; Amazon's customer reviews are also an excellent resource.

Size. Generally, halogen ovens come in 10 litre up to 17 litre capacities. We would advise opting for a larger capacity model if your budget can stretch, as this will allow you to cook for more people if needed.

Lid. The lid of a halogen cooker is what houses the cooking element. It can be quite heavy, and the element is extremely hot when the lid is lifted off after cooking - always use oven gloves. Most models should come with a lid rack, which enables you to place the lid on your countertop (otherwise the element would burn the work surface). If your budget can stretch, buying a model that has a hinged lid is easier and safer as it does not detach from the appliance.

Extras. It is worth researching which manufacturers will offer some handy extras. As standard, you should get a low and high rack with your appliance, but some also offer tongs, extender rings, recipe books and replacement bulbs. Always check the length of guarantee provided with each model.

Tips

• If your model has an extender ring, consider using it so that the element is further away from your food. For dishes that could potentially splash while cooking, this prevents the element from becoming dirty. The element can be difficult to clean so this will keep things manageable. Always wipe down the element when cooled with a damp cloth after cooking.
• Make sure you have enough space on your work surface. Although halogen ovens are relatively compact, if you do not own the model with a hinged lid you will have to allow space to remove the lid onto the lid stand.

• Use foil to prevent food from browning too quickly. This is not always necessary but can be a good way to prevent food from burning. Alternatively the extender ring can serve the same purpose by placing the element further from the food (but may result in longer cooking times).

• Be prepared to adjust cooking times. Groceries are rarely uniform in size and each model of halogen may be slightly different, so increasing or decreasing your oven temperatures and cooking times may be needed.

• Ensure you have the right sized dishes to fit your halogen oven before you begin cooking. Some recipes require ingredients to be placed in an ovenproof dish or baking tray rather than directly on the cooking racks.

• Consider which rack to use – low or high. If you need your food to brown, the high rack will be best but if you require longer cooking times, use the low rack. All our recipes specify which should be used.

• Lay some tin foil on the base of your bowl to catch any cooking juices. This will make washing up much easier.

• Make use of the self-clean function if your model has it. It will help remove any stubborn stains. The glass bowl is dishwasher-safe however never immerse the lid in water or any liquid. This can be wiped clean with a damp cloth only when cooled.

• Always read the manufacturer's instructions. These will offer some additional tips and safety guidelines to get the most out of your particular appliance.

• Some of our recipes may require the use of a hob for sautéing/browning, but we have kept this to a minimum.

We hope that this handy introduction will help you to get the most out of your halogen oven and that you find our recipes tasty and simple to follow. Have fun creating your meals and, as you gain confidence, create your own halogen show-stoppers for family and friends!

SWEET CHICKEN & SALAD WRAP

SERVES 4

Ingredients

- 120ml chicken stock
- 3 garlic cloves, crushed
- 1tbsp runny honey
- 1tbsp tomato purée
- ½tsp each mustard powder & ginger
- 4 chicken breasts, cubed
- 2tbsp soy sauce
- 4 low tortilla wraps
- 1 iceberg lettuce, shredded
- 4 ripe tomatoes, chopped
- 4tbsp soured cream
- Salt & pepper to season

Method

1. Mix together the stock, garlic, soy sauce, honey, tomato purée and ground spices.

2. Combine with chicken pieces in an ovenproof dish. Season, cover with foil and place on the lower rack of the halogen oven.

3. Leave to cook for 15-20 minutes at 200C/400F or until the chicken is cooked through.

4. Serve the chicken loaded in each tortilla wrap with the lettuce, tomatoes and soured cream.

PARMESAN PASTA SALAD

SERVES 4

Ingredients

- 400g farfalle pasta
- 2tbsp green pesto
- 4 chicken breasts
- 150g asparagus, chopped
- 2tbsp mayonnaise
- 2tbsp Parmesan cheese, grated
- Salt & pepper to season

Method

1. Boil the pasta in salted water until tender.

2. Drain, mix with the pesto and leave to cool.

3. Meanwhile combine the mayonnaise & Parmesan together. Smother over the chicken breasts and asparagus in an ovenproof dish.

4. Season, cover with foil and place on the lower rack of the halogen oven at 200C/400F for 25-30 minutes or until the chicken is cooked through.

5. Serve with the cooled pesto pasta on the side.

SMOTHERED PEANUT BUTTER CHICKEN

SERVES 4

Ingredients

- 2tsp each, paprika, cumin & coriander
- 4tbsp smooth peanut butter
- 4 chicken breasts
- 4 red peppers, sliced
- 2 onions, chopped
- 4tbsp lime juice
- 250ml chicken stock
- 2tbsp soy sauce
- 400g long grain rice
- Salt & pepper to season

Method

1. Mix the ground spices and peanut butter together to form a paste.

2. Score the chicken breasts with a knife and smother in the peanut paste.

3. Add all the ingredients, except the rice, to an ovenproof dish and cover with foil.

4. Place on the lower rack and leave to cook in the halogen oven at 200C/400F for 25-30 minutes or until the chicken is cooked through.

5. Meanwhile cook the rice in salted boiling water until tender.

6. Slice the chicken breast into thick slices, place on top of the rice and pour the peppers and stock over the top of the chicken.

CHICKEN & SAFFRON RICE

Ingredients

- 2tsp ground cinnamon
- 1tsp each paprika, cumin & coriander
- ½tsp nutmeg
- 2 garlic cloves, crushed
- 1tbsp olive oil
- 4 chicken breasts
- 400g Basmati rice
- 200g peas
- Large pinch of saffron
- Salt & pepper to season

Method

1. Mix the ground spices and garlic together with the olive oil to form a paste.

2. Score the chicken breasts with a knife and smother each in the spice paste.

3. Place on the lower rack, cover with foil and leave to cook in the halogen oven at 200C/400F for 25-30 minutes, or until the chicken is cooked through.

4. Meanwhile cook the rice and peas separately in salted boiling water (add the saffron to the rice pan while cooking)

5. Toss the rice and peas together and serve with the chicken.

HONEY CHICKEN & VEG

SERVES 4

Ingredients

- 4 garlic cloves, crushed
- 3tbsp lemon juice
- 2tbsp runny honey
- 1tbsp olive oil
- 4tsp soy sauce
- 500g sweet potatoes, cubed
- 4 parsnips, diced
- 4 carrots, sliced
- 2 onions, sliced
- 4 chicken breasts, cubed
- 200g tomatoes, halved
- Salt & pepper to season

Method

1. Mix together the garlic, lemon juice, honey, olive oil and soy sauce.
2. Brush the chicken, tomatoes & vegetables with the honey mixture.
3. Place the vegetables in an ovenproof dish and season well.
4. Cover with foil and place on the lower rack of the halogen oven at 200C/400F for 20 minutes.
5. Add the chicken and tomatoes to the dish and cook for a further 15-20 minutes or until the chicken is cooked through and the vegetables are tender.

BUTTER BEAN CHICKEN STEW

SERVES 4

Ingredients

- 2 onions, chopped
- 2 peppers, sliced
- 3 garlic cloves, crushed
- 1tbsp dried mixed herbs
- 1tbsp olive oil
- 1 small tin (200g) chopped tomatoes
- 4 chicken breasts, sliced
- 1 tin (400g) butter beans, drained
- 3tbsp Worcestershire sauce
- 3tbsp tomato purée
- Salt & pepper to season

Method

1. Gently sauté the onion, sliced pepper, garlic & herbs in the olive oil for a few minutes until softened.
2. Add the chopped tomatoes and sliced chicken and cook for 3-4 minutes longer.
3. Combine all the ingredients in an ovenproof dish. Cover with foil.
4. Place on the lower rack and leave to cook in the halogen oven at 200C/400F for 25-30 minutes or until the chicken is cooked through.
5. Season well and serve.

CREAMY MINT CHICKEN & NEW POTATOES

SERVES 4

Ingredients

- 2 onions, chopped
- 1tbsp olive oil
- 250ml chicken stock
- 3tbsp Dijon mustard
- 4 chicken breasts
- 400g new potatoes, sliced
- 100g spinach leaves
- 2tbsp crème fraiche
- 2tbsp fresh mint, chopped
- Salt & pepper to season

Method

1. Slice the chicken breasts into strips.

2. Gently sauté the onions in the oil for a few minutes.

3. Add the chicken stock and mustard to the pan and bring to the boil. Continue stirring for a minute or two while it bubbles away.

4. Combine all the ingredients, except the crème fraiche and chopped mint, in an ovenproof dish.

5. Place on the lower rack and leave to cook in the halogen oven at 180C/350F for 20-25 minutes or until the chicken is cooked through and the potatoes are tender.

6. After cooking gently stir through the crème fraiche, season and serve with the chopped mint sprinkled over the top.

TARRAGON CHICKEN SALAD

SERVES 4

Ingredients

- 4 lemons
- 4 garlic cloves, crushed
- 2tbsp fresh tarragon, chopped
- 1tsp crushed chilli flakes
- 4 chicken breasts
- 150g salad leaves
- 4 large plum tomatoes, sliced
- 2tbsp balsamic vinegar
- 2tbsp Parmesan shavings
- Salt & pepper to season

Method

1. Chop two of the lemons into slices. Squeeze and reserve the juice from the other two.

2. Combine the lemon juice, garlic, tarragon and chilli flakes together to create a marinade.

3. Place the chicken breasts in an ovenproof dish and score the flesh of each with a knife.

4. Brush the breasts evenly with all the marinade, season well and leave for up to 1 hour to marinate.

5. Carefully cover the chicken breasts with the sliced lemon pieces, place on the lower rack and leave to cook in the halogen oven for 25-30 minutes at 200C/400F or until the chicken breasts are cooked through.

6. Meanwhile toss together the salad leaves, plum tomatoes, and vinegar.

7. Serve the chicken with salad and Parmesan shavings.

TRIPLE CHEESE LASAGNE

SERVES 4+

Ingredients

- 800g chicken mince
- 1 onion, chopped
- 3 garlic cloves, crushed
- 1tbsp olive oil
- 1 tin (400g) chopped tomatoes
- 2tbsp tomato purée
- ½tsp salt
- 1tbsp Worcestershire sauce
- 2tsp dried mixed herbs
- 150g Ricotta cheese
- 150g Mozzarella cheese, grated
- 2 eggs, beaten
- 250g fresh lasagne sheets
- 150g Cheddar cheese, grated

Method

1. Gently sauté the chicken mince, onion and garlic in the olive oil for a few minutes.

2. Add the chopped tomatoes, puree, salt, Worcestershire sauce and mixed herbs. Cook for 4-5 minutes.

3. Meanwhile combine the Ricotta, Mozzarella and eggs together.

4. In an ovenproof dish, layer in turn the lasagne sheets, meat and cheese mix, finishing with a layer of meat on top sprinkled with the grated cheddar cheese.

5. Place on the lower rack of the halogen oven, cover with foil and cook at 200C/400F for 30-40 minutes or until cooked through.

6. Remove the foil for the last 10 minutes of cooking to brown the cheese before serving.

CHICKEN FAJITAS

Ingredients

- Cooking oil spray
- 2tsp each chilli powder, cumin, paprika, garlic & oregano
- 2tbsp lime juice
- 4 chicken breasts, sliced into strips
- 1 onion, sliced
- 3 red peppers, sliced
- 1tbsp olive oil
- 60ml chicken stock
- 1 Romaine lettuce shredded
- 4 tomatoes, chopped
- 4tbsp soured cream
- 1 avocado diced
- 4 flour tortilla wraps
- Salt & pepper to season

Method

1. Combine the dried spices and lime juice together with the chicken strips. Season, cover and leave to chill for an hour or two.

2. Meanwhile sauté the onion & peppers in the olive oil for a few minutes.

3. Place the chicken, onion, peppers and stock in an ovenproof dish.

4. Put on the lower rack of the halogen oven and cook at 200C/400F for 20-30 minutes or until the chicken is cooked through.

5. Spoon in to flour tortillas. Add the salad, soured cream and avocado. Fold & enjoy.

CHICKEN GOUJONS

SERVES 4

Ingredients

- 3 slices white bread
- 2tsp paprika
- 3 garlic, clove
- 3tbsp grated Parmesan cheese
- 150g plain flour
- 3 free range eggs
- 4 chicken breasts, cut into strips
- Cooking oil spray
- 4 wholemeal soft rolls
- 2tbsp mayonnaise
- 1 lemon cut into wedges
- Salt & pepper to season

Method

1. First make the breadcrumbs by whizzing the bread, paprika, garlic and cheese in a food processor for a few seconds.

2. Sieve the flour onto a plate. Put the breadcrumbs on a separate plate and beat the eggs in a bowl. Cover each chicken strip with flour by rolling them on the flour plate and then dip each strip in the egg. Coat well in the breadcrumbs.

3. Spray with cooking oil and place on the lower rack of the halogen oven on 200C/400F for 10-15 minutes or until the chicken is cooked through and the goujons are golden brown

4. Split the rolls and spread with mayonnaise, add the goujons and serve with lemon wedges.

CHICKEN KORMA

Ingredients

- 4 chicken breasts, cubed
- 1 onion, chopped
- 1tbsp olive oil
- 3tbsp mild curry powder
- 1 400g tin chopped tomatoes
- ½tsp salt
- 1tsp brown sugar
- 3tbsp tomato purée
- 2tbsp ground almonds
- 120ml coconut milk
- 400g Basmati rice
- Salt & pepper to season

Method

1. Brown the chicken and onions for a few minutes in a frying pan with the olive oil.

2. Add the curry powder and gently cook for a minute or two.

3. Put in an ovenproof dish and add the chopped tomatoes, salt, sugar, puree and ground almonds.

4. Place on the lower rack and leave to cook in the halogen oven at 200C/400F for 15-20 minutes or until the chicken is cooked through.

5. Meanwhile rinse the rice in a sieve with cold water and cook in a pan of salted boiling water until tender.

6. Stir the coconut milk through and serve.

LEMON & THYME CHICKEN

SERVES 2

Ingredients

- 2 lemons
- 2 garlic cloves, crushed
- 1tbsp fresh thyme, chopped
- Large pinch of crushed chilli flakes
- 2 chicken breasts
- Large handful of rocket leaves
- 2tsp olive oil
- 1tbsp Parmesan shavings
- Salt & pepper to season

Method

1. Thinly slice one of the lemons. Squeeze and reserve the juice from the other.

2. Combine the lemon juice, garlic, thyme and chilli flakes together to create a marinade.

3. Place the chicken breasts in an ovenproof dish and score the flesh with a knife.

4. Brush the breasts with the marinade, season well and leave for an hour to marinate.

5. Carefully cover the chicken breast with the lemon slices, place on the lower rack and leave to cook in the halogen oven for 25-30 minutes at 200C/400F or until the chicken is cooked through.

6. Remove the cooked chicken to a plate and serve alongside the rocket dressed with olive oil and Parmesan shavings.

COCONUT CHICKEN WITH RICE

SERVES 2

Ingredients

- 2 onions, chopped
- 2 garlic cloves, crushed
- 2tsp fresh ginger, grated
- ½tsp cinnamon
- 1tsp cayenne pepper
- 1tsp each paprika & mustard seeds
- 2tsp olive oil
- 2 chicken breasts
- 2 medium sweet potatoes, thinly sliced
- 2tsp plain flour
- 120ml hot chicken stock
- 200g long grain rice
- 120ml coconut milk
- Salt & pepper to season

Method

1. Gently sauté the onion, garlic, ginger, dried spices and mustard seeds in the olive oil for a few minutes.

2. Stir through the flour and add the hot chicken stock to the pan. Continue stirring for a minute or two.

3. Combine all the ingredients, except the rice and coconut milk in an ovenproof dish.

4. Place the dish on the lower rack, cover with foil and leave to cook in the halogen oven at 180C/350F for 30-35 minutes or until the chicken is cooked through and the sweet potato is tender.

5. Meanwhile cook the rice in salted boiling water until tender.

6. When the chicken is cooked, stir through the coconut milk. Season and serve with the boiled rice.

PESTO CHICKEN

Ingredients

- 2 chicken breasts
- 2tbsp green pesto
- 2 red onions, sliced
- 150g green beans
- 150g baby corn
- 2tsp oregano
- 1tbsp olive oil
- Salt & pepper to season

Method

1. Hold the chicken breast as if you were slicing through the centre of it to butterfly it. Stop slicing before you cut it in half completely, open the chicken breast to expose the two inside parts.

2. Spread the inside with pesto and close your 'sandwich' back up so you are left with pesto through the centre of the chicken breast.

3. Place the chicken, onions and vegetables in an ovenproof dish. Season well, brush with olive oil, sprinkle with the dried oregano and cover with foil.

4. Place on the lower rack and leave to cook in the halogen oven at 200C/400F for 25-30 minutes or until the chicken is cooked through and the vegetables are tender.

5. Remove from the halogen oven and arrange the beans, corn and onions as a bed onto which you serve the pesto chicken breast.

CREAMY MUSTARD CHICKEN

SERVES 2

Ingredients

- 2 chicken breasts
- 2 onions, chopped
- 150g mushrooms, sliced
- 2tsp olive oil
- 100ml chicken stock
- 1tbsp Dijon mustard
- 300g small new potatoes, halved
- 75g spinach leaves
- 3tbsp crème fraiche
- 1tbsp fresh parsley, chopped
- Salt & pepper to season

Method

1. Slice the chicken into strips. Gently sauté the onions and mushrooms in olive oil for a few minutes.

2. Add the chicken stock and mustard to the pan and bring to the boil.

3. Reduce the heat. Combine all the ingredients in an ovenproof dish.

4. Place on the lower rack and leave to cook in the halogen oven at 180C/350F for 30-35 minutes or until the chicken is cooked through and the potatoes are tender.

5. After cooking gently stir through the crème fraiche, season and serve with chopped parsley sprinkled over the top.

SPANISH CHICKEN

SERVES 2

Ingredients

- 1 onion, chopped
- 1 yellow pepper, sliced
- 2 garlic cloves, crushed
- 1tsp smoked paprika
- 2tsp olive oil
- 1tsp sage
- 200g uncooked chorizo sausage, sliced
- 2 chicken breasts, sliced
- 1 tin (400g) chopped tomatoes
- 200g tender stem broccoli, roughly chopped
- Handful fresh basil leaves
- Salt & pepper to season

Method

1. Gently sauté the onion, sliced pepper, garlic & paprika in the olive oil for a few minutes until softened.
2. Add the sliced chorizo & chicken and cook for 3-4 minutes longer.
3. Combine all the ingredients, except the fresh basil, in an ovenproof dish and cover with foil.
4. Place on the lower rack and leave to cook in the halogen oven at 200C/400F for 25-30 minutes or until the chicken is cooked through and the vegetables are tender.
5. Season well and serve with torn basil leaves over the top.

CHICKEN & SERRANO HAM

SERVES 2

Ingredients

- 2 chicken breasts
- 2tbsp cream cheese with chives
- 4 slices Serrano ham
- 12 ripe plum tomatoes, halved
- 1tbsp garlic oil (or mix a little olive oil with crushed garlic)
- 100g spinach leaves
- Salt & pepper to season

Method

1. Make a lengthways slit in each chicken breast and stuff with cream cheese. Season the chicken breast and wrap with the Serrano ham (secure in place with a cocktail stick skewered through each breast).

2. Place in an ovenproof dish on the lower rack. Cover with foil and leave to cook in the halogen oven at 200C/400F for 25-30 minutes or until the chicken is cooked through. Meanwhile mix together the tomatoes, garlic oil and spinach leaves so that they all have a thin coating of oil on them.

3. Season well and arrange around the chicken in the ovenproof dish 10 minutes before the end of cooking time. Ensure the chicken and vegetables are cooked through before serving.

SUNDRIED TOMATO CHICKEN

Ingredients

- 2tbsp strong soft cheese (such as Boursin)
- 1tsp anchovy paste
- 2 chicken breasts
- 2tbsp sundried tomato paste
- 300g broccoli florets
- Salt & pepper to season

Method

1. First mix together the cheese and anchovy paste.

2. Hold each chicken breast as if you were slicing through the centre of it to butterfly it. Stop slicing before you cut it in half completely and open the chicken breast to expose the two inside parts. Spread the inside of each chicken breast with the anchovy & cheese mix and close your 'sandwich' breast back up.

3. Spread the top of the chicken with the sundried tomato paste and cover with foil.

4. Place in an ovenproof dish on the lower rack and leave to cook in the halogen oven at 200C/400F for 25-30 minutes or until the chicken is cooked through. Meanwhile steam the broccoli florets over a pan of boiling water for 5-10 minutes or until tender.

5. Season well and serve.

NUTTY CHICKEN

SERVES 2

Ingredients

- 1tbsp ground almonds
- 2tbsp walnuts, finely chopped
- 100g chestnut mushrooms, chopped
- 1 onion, finely chopped
- 2 garlic cloves, crushed
- 2tsp olive oil
- 2 chicken breasts
- 300g new potatoes
- Salt & pepper to season

Method

1. First combine together the ground almonds, walnuts, mushrooms, onion, garlic & olive oil.

2. Make a lengthways slit in the chicken breast and stuff with the walnut mixture. Don't worry if it's overflowing, just gently cover in foil to keep it together.

3. Place in an ovenproof dish on the lower rack and leave to cook in the halogen oven at 200C/400F for 25-30 minutes or until the chicken is cooked through. Meanwhile steam the new potatoes in a pan of boiling water for 10-20 minutes or until tender.

4. Season well and serve.

TURKEY BURGERS

Ingredients

- 2 slices brown bread
- 2 garlic cloves
- 1 onion
- 800g turkey mince
- 3 egg yolks
- 1tbsp olive oil
- 2 ripe tomatoes, sliced
- 1 iceberg lettuce, shredded
- 4 brioche burger rolls
- Mayonnaise & mustard to serve
- Salt & pepper to season

Method

1. Place the bread and garlic in a food processor and pulse to make breadcrumbs. Add the onion and whizz again. Add the turkey mince and egg yolk and pulse for a few seconds longer until combined.
2. Season well and form into four burger patties.
3. Brush with olive oil and place on the lower rack of the halogen oven on 240C/475F.
4. Grill for 6-8 minutes each side, or until the burgers are cooked through.
5. Serve with sliced tomato and lettuce, mayonnaise and mustard.

EASY SPICED KEBABS

Ingredients

- 2 chicken breasts, cubed
- 2tbsp Greek yoghurt
- 2tbsp curry powder
- 2 garlic cloves, crushed
- 4 metal skewers
- 2 Romaine lettuce, shredded
- 1 red onion, sliced
- 1 lemon cut into wedges
- Salt & pepper to season

Method

1. Season the cubed chicken.

2. Mix together the yoghurt, curry powder and garlic.

3. Combine well with the chicken, cover and leave to chill for an hour or two.

4. Skewer the chicken pieces to make 4 chicken kebabs and place on the lower rack of the halogen oven on 240C/475F.

5. Grill for 6-8 minutes each side or until the chicken is cooked through (take care handling the skewers as they will get hot).

6. Serve with the shredded lettuce, sliced onions and lemon wedges.

CHICKEN & CANNELLINI BEANS

SERVES 2

Ingredients

- 1 onion, chopped
- 2 red peppers, sliced
- 2 garlic cloves, crushed
- 2tsp dried mixed herbs
- 2tsp olive oil
- 1 tin (400g) chopped tomatoes
- 2 chicken breasts, sliced diagonally
- 1 tin (400g) cannellini beans, drained
- 2tbsp Worcestershire sauce
- 2tbsp tomato purée
- Salt & pepper to season

Method

1. Gently sauté the onions, sliced peppers, garlic & herbs in olive oil for a few minutes until softened.

2. Add the chopped tomatoes and sliced chicken and cook for 3-4 minutes longer. Combine all the ingredients in an ovenproof dish and cover with foil.

3. Place on the lower rack and leave to cook in the halogen oven at 200C/400F for 25-30 minutes or until the chicken is cooked through.

4. Season well and serve.

TANDOORI PITTA CHICKEN

SERVES 2

Ingredients

- 2tsp each cumin, turmeric, coriander & chilli powder
- 1tsp each ginger & garam masala
- 2 garlic cloves, crushed
- 1tbsp olive oil
- 2 chicken breasts, cubed
- 2tbsp Greek yoghurt
- 2tsp mint sauce
- 1 lemon cut into wedges
- 1 baby gem lettuce, shredded
- 1 red onion, sliced
- 2 large pitta bread
- Salt & pepper to season

Method

1. Mix together the ground spices, garlic and olive oil to form a paste.
2. Season the chicken and smother in the spice paste.
3. Place in an ovenproof dish and leave for up to 1 hour to marinate.
4. Cover with foil, place on the lower rack and leave to cook in the halogen oven for 25-30 minutes at 200C/400F or until the chicken is cooked through.
5. Meanwhile mix the mint sauce and Greek yoghurt together.
6. When the chicken is cooked through squeeze a little lemon juice over the top.
7. Stuff the pitta breads with the chicken, lettuce & onion and serve the lemon wedges and mint yoghurt on the side.

BUTTER ROAST CHICKEN

SERVES 4+

Ingredients

- 100g butter
- 2 garlic cloves, crushed
- 1tbsp fresh basil, chopped
- 1.75kg chicken
- 4 streaky bacon rashers
- Salt & pepper to season

Method

1. Combine together the butter, garlic and basil to make a herb butter.

2. Use your hands to force the herb butter underneath the skin of the chicken breast evenly, to give as much of the bird as possible a good covering.

3. Season well.

4. Lay the streaky bacon rashers over the breast, cover with foil and place on the lower rack of the halogen oven.

5. Cook for 75 minutes at 180C/350F.

6. Remove the foil, increase the heat to 200C/400F and cook for a further 15 minutes for or until the chicken is cooked through.

CHORIZO OMELETTE

Ingredients

- 4 onions
- 800g potatoes
- 1tbsp olive oil
- 6 free range eggs
- 150g chorizo sausage, chopped
- 200g mixed salad leaves
- Mayonnaise to serve
- Salt & pepper to season

Method

1. In a food processor whizz together the unpeeled potatoes and onion, then gently sauté in a frying pan with the olive oil for 10 minutes until softened.

2. Beat the eggs and combine with the sautéed mixture in a shallow greased ovenproof dish.

3. Season well, cover with foil and place on the lower rack and cook in the halogen oven at 200C/400F for 25-35 minutes or until the omelette is firm.

4. Cut into wedges and serve with mixed salad leaves and mayo on the side.

GNOCCHI & SAUSAGE BAKE

SERVES 4

Ingredients

- 2 onions, chopped
- 12 pork sausages, sliced
- 1tbsp olive oil
- 2tbsp Worcestershire sauce
- 250ml passata
- 2tsp rosemary
- 1tsp brown sugar
- ½tsp salt
- 1 tin (400g) chopped tomatoes
- 200g spinach
- 1kg gnocchi
- Salt & pepper to season

Method

1. Gently brown the onions and sliced sausages in a frying pan with the olive oil for a few minutes.

2. Place in an ovenproof dish with all the ingredients and mix well.

3. Cover and cook on the lower rack of the halogen oven at 200C/400F for 20-25 minutes or until the sausages are cooked through and the gnocchi dumplings are tender.

HONEY PORK NOODLES

SERVES 4

Ingredients

- 500ml pork tenderloin, cubed
- 1tbsp olive oil
- 2 onions, chopped
- 3 garlic cloves, crushed
- 1tbsp runny honey
- 1tbsp soy sauce
- 1tbsp tomato purée
- 120ml chicken stock
- 2 pak choi, shredded
- 1tbsp sesame seeds
- 1 large bunch spring onions, chopped
- 2 limes, cut into wedges
- 400g egg noodles
- Salt & pepper to season

Method

1. Season the pork and quickly brown in a hot frying pan for a few minutes with the olive oil.

2. Remove the pork and use the same pan to gently sauté the onions and garlic for a few minutes.

3. Place everything, except the sesame seeds, spring onions, lime wedges and noodles into an ovenproof dish.

4. Cover with foil and cook on the lower rack of the halogen oven at 200C/400F for 20-25 minutes or until the pork is cooked through.

5. Meanwhile cook the noodles in boiling salted water until tender.

6. When the pork is cooked, season and serve on a bed of noodles with the sesame seeds & spring onions sprinkled over the top and lime wedges on the side.

MINI LAMB BURGERS

SERVES 4

Ingredients

- 2 onions, chopped
- 1 green chilli, finely chopped
- 2tsp each coriander, paprika, cumin & turmeric
- 2 garlic cloves, crushed
- 1tbsp olive oil
- 800g lamb mince
- 2tbsp fresh mint, chopped
- 1tbsp lemon juice
- 4 large pitta bread
- 2 romaine lettuces, shredded
- 4 tomatoes, finely chopped
- 2tbsp Greek yoghurt
- 2tsp mint sauce
- Salt & pepper to season

Method

1. Gently sauté the onion, green chilli, coriander, paprika, cumin, turmeric and garlic in the olive oil for a few minutes. Season well.

2. Place the mince, lemon juice, chopped mint and warm spicy onion mixture into a food processor and whizz together.

3. Take the mixture out, divide into 20-24 portions and shape into small flat meat patties.

4. Spray with a little cooking oil and place on the grill rack at the bottom of the halogen oven on 240C/475F. Grill for 6-8 minutes each side or until the lamb is properly cooked through.

5. Serve inside the pitta bread with the lettuce, tomatoes, yoghurt and mint sauce.

LAMB CHAPATTIS

SERVES 4

Ingredients

- 750g lamb mince
- 1tbsp olive oil
- 3tbsp balsamic vinegar
- 1tsp each garam masala, turmeric, coriander
- 2 garlic cloves, crushed
- 2 carrots, diced
- 1 red onion, chopped
- 1tbsp mint sauce
- 200g peas
- 120ml lamb stock
- 4 chapatti bread wraps
- Salt & pepper to season

Method

1. Season the lamb and quickly brown in a frying pan for a few minutes with the olive oil.

2. Place in an ovenproof dish with all the other ingredients, except the chapatti bread.

3. Cover with foil and cook on the lower rack of the halogen oven at 200C/400F for 30-40 minutes or until the lamb is cooked through and the carrots are tender. Serve with the chapatti bread on the side.

CHOCOLATE CHILLI BEEF

SERVES 4

Ingredients

- 800g beef mince
- 2 onions, chopped
- 4 carrots, finely diced
- 2 garlic cloves, crushed
- 2tsp cumin
- 1tsp chilli powder
- 1tbsp olive oil
- 2tbsp cocoa powder
- 1 tin (200g) chopped tomatoes
- 2tbsp sundried tomato purée
- 250ml beef stock
- 8 taco shells
- 4tbsp soured cream
- 2 baby gem lettuce, shredded
- 1 avocado diced

Method

1. Brown the mince and gently sauté the onions, carrots, garlic and spices in the olive oil for a few minutes.

2. Add the cocoa powder, tomatoes, puree and beef stock. Cook for 4-5 minutes longer and put into an ovenproof dish.

3. Place on the lower rack and leave to cook in the halogen oven at 200C/400F for 20-25 minutes or until the mince is cooked through and the stock is absorbed.

4. Season well and serve with the taco shells, soured cream, shredded lettuce and avocado.

PORK LOIN STEAKS & APPLE

Ingredients

- 4 pork loin steaks
- 4 apples, chopped
- 4 garlic cloves, crushed
- 300g mushrooms, sliced
- 2tsp olive oil
- 120ml apple juice
- 3tbsp crème fraiche
- 300g shredded vegetable ribbons
- Cooking oil spray
- Salt & pepper to season

Method

1. Season the pork loin steaks. Spray with a little cooking oil and place in an ovenproof dish at the top of the halogen oven at 240C/475F. Grill for 3-4 mins each side.

2. Meanwhile gently sauté the chopped apples, garlic and mushrooms in the olive oil for a few minutes until softened.

3. Stir through the apple juice & crème fraiche and pour over the pork steaks (use the same pan for the vegetables later).

4. Reduce the heat in the halogen oven to 200C/400F and cook for a further 6-8 minutes or until the pork is cooked through.

5. Meanwhile use the same pan to gently sauté the vegetable ribbons for a few minutes in any leftover juices from the mushroom mixture.

6. Season well and serve.

SPANISH SAUSAGE CASSEROLE

SERVES 4

Ingredients

- 2 onions, chopped
- 4 peppers, sliced
- 2 garlic cloves, crushed
- 2tsp dried mixed herbs
- 1tbsp olive oil
- 8 pork sausages, sliced
- 200g chorizo, sliced
- 1 tin (400g) chopped tomatoes
- 1 tin (400g) mixed beans, drained
- 2tbsp Worcestershire sauce
- 3tbsp tomato purée
- Salt & pepper to season

Method

1. Gently sauté the onion, sliced peppers, garlic & herbs in olive oil for a few minutes until softened.

2. Add the sausages and chorizo and cook for 4-5 minutes longer.

3. Combine all the ingredients in an ovenproof dish. Place on the lower rack and leave to cook in the halogen oven at 200C/400F for 30-40 minutes or until the sausages are cooked through and the beans are tender.

4. Season well and serve.

CREAMY BEEF STROGANOFF & RICE

SERVES 4

Ingredients

- 2 onions, chopped
- 3 garlic cloves, crushed
- 300g mushrooms, sliced
- 1tbsp olive oil
- 800g sirloin steak, cut into fine strips
- 2tsp each oregano & tarragon
- 1tbsp Dijon mustard
- 60ml beef stock
- 5tbsp crème fraiche
- 400g long grain rice
- 2tbsp fresh flat leaf parsley, chopped
- Salt & pepper to season

Method

1. Gently sauté the onions, garlic & mushrooms in the olive oil for a few minutes.

2. Add the steak and cook for 3-4 minutes longer.

3. Place all the ingredients, except the rice, in an ovenproof dish and combine well. Place on the lower rack, cover and leave to cook in the halogen oven at 200C/400F for 10-15 minutes or until the sauce is creamy & the steak is tender and cooked through (add a little more crème fraiche or stock if needed). Meanwhile cook the rice in salted boiling water until tender.

4. Season well and serve with the stroganoff piled on top of a bed of rice.

SPAGHETTI & MEATBALLS

SERVES 4

Ingredients

- 2 slices brown bread
- 2 garlic cloves
- 1 onion
- 600g beef mince
- 2tsp each cumin, turmeric, paprika & basil
- 2 free range eggs
- 500ml tomato passata
- 2tbsp tomato purée
- 2tbsp Worcestershire sauce
- 1tsp each salt & brown sugar
- 375g spaghetti
- Cooking oil spray
- Salt & pepper to season

Method

1. Place the bread and garlic in a food processor and pulse to make breadcrumbs. Add the onion and whizz again. Add the mince, spices, herbs & eggs and pulse for a few seconds longer until well combined.

2. Season well and form into small meatballs with your hands.

3. Place in an ovenproof dish cooking, spray with a little oil and place on the lower rack in the halogen oven at 200C/400F for 10-15 minutes.

4. Combine together the passata, purée, Worcestershire sauce, salt & sugar. Add to the meatballs, mix well and continue to cook for a further 15-20 minutes until the meatballs are cooked through and the sauce is piping hot.

5. Meanwhile cook the spaghetti in salted boiling water until tender.

6. Serve with the meatballs and sauce piled on top of the spaghetti.

HAM & LEEK BAKE

SERVES 4

Ingredients

- 4 garlic cloves, crushed
- 700g potatoes, peeled & cubed
- 4 leeks, sliced
- 1tbsp olive oil
- 2tbsp butter spread
- 2tbsp plain flour
- 500ml milk
- 200g Cheddar cheese, grated
- 1tbsp Dijon mustard
- 400g thick ham, chopped
- 250g fresh breadcrumbs
- 2tbsp fresh parsley, chopped
- 1 head broccoli, roughly chopped
- Salt & pepper to season

Method

1. Gently sauté the garlic, potatoes, leeks and olive oil for a few minutes until softened.

2. Gently heat the butter in a saucepan and add the flour, stirring continuously to create a roux. Slowly add the milk and carry on stirring to prevent lumps. Warm through until the sauce thickens a little.

3. Combine all the ingredients in an ovenproof dish and sprinkle the breadcrumbs on top.

4. Place on the lower rack and leave to cook in the halogen oven at 200C/400F for 30-35 minutes or until the vegetables are tender. Season well and serve.

MOUSSAKA

SERVES 4

Ingredients

- 2 onions, chopped
- 700g lean lamb mince
- 2 aubergines, sliced
- 3 garlic cloves, crushed
- 2tsp oregano
- ½tsp nutmeg
- 1tbsp olive oil
- 1 tin (400g) chopped tomatoes
- 3tbsp tomato purée
- 500ml Greek yoghurt
- 300g Cheddar cheese, grated
- 500g potatoes, thinly sliced
- Salt & pepper to season

Method

1. Gently sauté the onion, garlic, aubergines, garlic, oregano & spices in the olive oil for a few minutes until softened. Add the chopped tomatoes, puree & lamb mince and cook for 3-4 minutes longer.

2. Place all the ingredients, except the yoghurt, cheese and potatoes, in an ovenproof dish layering the aubergine slices on top. Cover with potato slices.

3. Meanwhile very gently heat the yoghurt and cheese together in a saucepan and, when combined, carefully pour over the top of the ovenproof dish.

4. Place on the lower rack, cover with foil and leave to cook in the halogen oven at 200C/400F for 30-40 minutes or until the lamb is cooked through and the potatoes are tender.

5. Uncover and leave to cook for a further 10 minutes to brown.

6. Season well and serve.

FRUITY LAMB CASSEROLE

SERVES 4

Ingredients

- 2 onions, chopped
- 2 garlic cloves, crushed
- 2tsp each cumin & coriander
- 1tsp each cinnamon & chilli powder
- 1tbsp olive oil
- 1 tin (400g) chopped tomatoes
- 500g lean lamb fillet, cubed
- 4 ripe peaches, stoned and cut into wedges
- 1 tin (400g) chickpeas, drained
- 3tbsp Worcestershire sauce
- 2tbsp tomato purée
- Salt & pepper to season

Method

1. Gently sauté the onion, garlic & spices in the olive oil for a few minutes until softened.

2. Add the chopped tomatoes and cubed lamb and cook for 3-4 minutes longer. Combine all the ingredients in an ovenproof dish.

3. Place on the lower rack, cover with foil and cook at 200C/400F for 40-50 minutes or until the lamb is tender and cooked through.

4. Season well and serve.

HOMEMADE BEEF BURGERS

SERVES 4

Ingredients

- 2 slices brown bread
- 4 garlic cloves
- 1 onion
- 500g beef mince
- 1tsp each cumin, turmeric & paprika
- 2tsp Dijon mustard
- 2 eggs
- 4 soft burger rolls
- 4 slices Cheddar cheese
- 1 iceberg lettuce, shredded
- 4 ripe tomatoes, sliced
- Ketchup & mayonnaise to serve
- Cooking oil spray
- Salt & pepper to season

Method

1. Place the bread and garlic in a food processor and pulse to make breadcrumbs. Add the onion and whizz again.

2. Add the mince, spices, mustard and eggs. Pulse for a few seconds longer until combined.

3. Season well and form into 4 large burger patties thick. Spray with a little cooking oil and place on the lower rack of the halogen oven at 240C/475F. Grill for 5-7 minutes each side, or until the burgers are cooked through.

4. Serve in rolls with the cheese, salad and sauce.

CITRUS PORK TENDERLOIN

SERVES 4

Ingredients

- 1kg pork tenderloin
- 1tbsp olive oil
- 120ml/½ cup chicken stock
- 120ml/½ cup fresh orange juice
- 4 garlic cloves, crushed
- 4tbsp fresh sage, chopped
- 500g butternut squash, finely diced
- 200g spinach, chopped
- Salt & pepper to season

Method

1. Season the pork tenderloin and quickly brown in a frying pan for a few minutes with the olive oil.

2. Place in an ovenproof dish with all the other ingredients and cover with foil. Cook on the lower rack of the halogen oven at 200C/400F for 30-40 minutes or until the pork is cooked through and the squash is tender.

3. Remove the pork and cut into thick slices. Arrange on the plate with the spinach and squash to the side. Pour the juices over the top of the pork and vegetables to serve.

TOAD IN THE HOLE

SERVES 4

Ingredients

- 12 pork sausages
- 1tbsp olive oil
- 150g plain flour
- 2 eggs
- 175ml milk
- 2tsp Dijon mustard
- 1tsp thyme
- 1 tin (400g) baked beans
- Cooking oil spray
- Salt & pepper to season

Method

1. Pierce the sausages and put in an ovenproof dish with a little cooking oil spray. Cook on the lower rack of the halogen oven at 200C/400F for 8-12 minutes or until the sausages are browned.

2. Meanwhile make the batter by sifting the flour into a bowl. Beat the eggs into the flour and gradually add the milk, beating all the time to create a smooth batter.

3. Add the dried herbs, mustard and seasoning.

4. Pour the batter over the top of the sausages and cook for a further 25-35 minutes until the batter is golden brown and puffed up.

5. Heat the baked beans in a saucepan and serve with the toad in the hole.

STEAK & ONION PIE

SERVES 4

Ingredients

- 600g skirt steak, trimmed & cubed
- 1tbsp olive oil
- 2 onions, chopped
- 2 carrots, diced
- 125g mushrooms, chopped
- 120ml beef stock
- 1tbsp tomato purée
- 1tbsp Worcestershire sauce
- 2tsp corn-flour
- 375g ready made puff pastry
- Splash of milk
- 400g spring greens, shredded
- 1tbsp garlic oil (or mix a little oil with crushed garlic)
- Salt & pepper to season

Method

1. Brown the steak in a pan with the olive oil. Remove to a plate and gently sauté the onions, carrots and mushrooms for a few minutes.

2. Put the beef back into the pan, add the stock, puree and Worcestershire sauce. Stir and put into an ovenproof pie-dish. Season, cover and place on the lower rack of the halogen oven to cook at 180C/350F for 25-30 minutes or until the steak is tender and cooked through.

3. Place the corn-flour in a cup and add a little water to create a paste. Add the paste to the pie dish and stir through to thicken. Roll out the puff pastry and cover the meat. Push the edges down and trim off the sides. Brush with a little milk, increase the temperature to 200C/400F and bake for 10-15 minutes or until the pastry puffs up and is golden brown.. Meanwhile steam the spring greens for a few minutes. Dress with garlic oil, season, toss & serve with the steak pie.

SLOPPY JOES

Ingredients

- 500g mince beef
- 1tbsp olive oil
- 1 onion, chopped
- 2 garlic cloves, crushed
- 1 red pepper, sliced
- 1 tin (400g) chopped tomatoes
- 1tsp chilli powder, mustard powder & paprika
- 3tbsp BBQ sauce
- 4 burger rolls
- 125g Cheddar cheese, grated
- Salt & pepper to season

Method

1. Gently brown the beef in a frying pan with the olive oil and set to one side.

2. In the same pan sauté the onions, garlic and peppers for a few minutes.

3. Combine all the ingredients, except rolls and cheese, in an ovenproof dish. Season and cook on the lower rack of the halogen oven at 200C/400F for 25-35 minutes or until the beef is cooked through and the liquid has reduced.

4. Load the mince into the burger rolls with grated cheese piled on top.

SHEPHERD'S PIE

SERVES 4

Ingredients

- 700g potatoes, cubed
- Dash of milk & butter for mashing
- 750g lean minced lamb
- 1tbsp olive oil
- 1 onion, chopped
- 2 stalks celery & 2 carrots, diced
- 2 garlic cloves, crushed
- 2tsp mixed dried herbs
- 1tbsp plain flour
- 75g each mushrooms & peas,
- 1 tin (200g) chopped tomatoes
- 1tbsp Worcestershire sauce
- 120ml lamb stock
- 2tbsp tomato purée
- Salt & pepper to season

Method

1. Cook the potatoes in salted boiling water until tender. Mash into a smooth consistency with a little milk and butter.

2. Meanwhile brown the lamb in the olive oil. Remove from the pan and gently sauté the onions, celery, carrots, garlic and herbs for a few minutes in the same pan.

3. Discard any excess fat before stirring through the flour. Add all the other ingredients, except the mashed potato, to an ovenproof dish. Cover and cook on the lower rack of the halogen oven at 200C/400F for 20-25 minutes.

4. After this time cover evenly with the mashed potato and replace in the oven. Leave to cook for a further 15-20 minutes or until the meat is cooked through, the vegetables are tender and the mash is golden brown.

LAMB HOTPOT

Ingredients

- 700g lean lamb fillet, cubed
- 1tbsp olive oil
- 4 carrots, chopped
- 2 onions, chopped
- 2tbsp plain flour
- 500ml lamb stock
- 2tsp thyme
- 2tbsp tomato purée
- 1 bay leaf
- 2tbsp Worcestershire sauce
- 600g potatoes, peeled & thinly sliced
- Cooking oil spray
- Salt & pepper to season

Method

1. Brown the lamb in a frying pan with the olive oil and place in an ovenproof dish. Put to one side and gently sauté the carrots and onion in the same pan for a few minutes.

2. Add the flour and stir well, pour in the stock, thyme, tomato purée, bay leaf and Worcestershire sauce.

3. Bring to the boil, add the contents of the pan to the ovenproof dish and stir.

4. Arrange the potato slices over the top. Season well, spray with cooking oil and cover with foil.

5. Place on the lower rack of the halogen oven at 180C/350F and cook for 60-70 minutes or until the lamb is cooked through and the potato slices are tender. Remove the foil cover for the last 10 minutes of cooking to brown the potatoes.

BEAN & SAUSAGE BAKE

SERVES 4

Ingredients

- 12 pork sausages, sliced
- 1 onion, chopped
- 2 carrots, finely chopped
- 2tsp olive oil
- 1 tin (400g) mixed beans, drained
- 1 tin (400g) chopped tomatoes
- 3tbsp tomato ketchup
- 2tsp Dijon mustard
- 60ml vegetable stock
- Salt & pepper to season

Method

1. Brown the sausage slices, onions and carrots in a frying pan with the olive oil for a few minutes.

2. Combine all the other ingredients in an ovenproof dish and season.

3. Place on the lower rack of the halogen oven at 200C/400F for 30-40 minutes or until the sausages are cooked through, the vegetables are tender and the stock is absorbed.

CORNED BEEF HASH BAKE

SERVES 4

Ingredients

- 1 onion, sliced
- ½ savoy cabbage, shredded
- 2 carrots, finely chopped
- 800g potatoes and diced
- 1tbsp olive oil
- 1 tin (340g) corned beef, cubed
- 100g peas
- ½tsp crushed chilli flakes
- 120ml beef stock
- Salt & pepper to season

Method

1. Gently sauté the onions, cabbage, carrots and potatoes in the olive oil for 10 minutes.

2. Season and combine all the ingredients in an ovenproof dish.

3. Place on the lower rack of the halogen oven on 200C/400F for 30-40 minutes or until the vegetables are tender and the stock is absorbed.

CHILLI & TORTILLA CHIPS

SERVES 4

Ingredients

- 700g minced beef
- 1 onion, chopped
- 1tbsp olive oil
- 2 garlic cloves, crushed
- 1tsp each brown sugar, oregano, cumin, mild chilli powder & paprika
- 1 tin (400g) chopped tomatoes
- 1 tin (400g) kidney beans, drained
- 120ml beef stock
- 120ml tomato passata
- 2tbsp tomato purée
- 4tbsp soured cream
- 2 red chillies, finely sliced
- 150g Cheddar cheese, grated
- Large bag chilli tortilla chips

Method

1. Brown the mince, onions, garlic sugar, spices and salt in a frying pan with the olive oil.

2. Drain off any excess oil. Combine all the ingredients, except the soured cream, chillies, cheese and tortilla chips, in an ovenproof dish. Cover with foil and place on the lower rack of the halogen oven on 200C/400F for 50-60 minutes or until the beef is cooked through.

3. Leave uncovered to cook for a further 10 minutes to reduce down the sauce if needed.

4. Serve with the soured cream, chillies, cheese and tortilla chips.

STEAK SANDWICH

SERVES 4

Ingredients

- 1 onion, sliced
- 2 red peppers, sliced
- 75g mushrooms, sliced
- 2tsp paprika
- 1tbsp Worcestershire sauce
- 1tbsp olive oil
- 4 frying steaks
- 4 cheese slices
- 1tbsp fresh oregano, chopped
- 4 submarine sandwich rolls
- Salt & pepper to season

Method

1. Gently sauté the onions, peppers and mushrooms in a frying pan with the paprika, Worcestershire sauce and olive oil for a few minutes.

2. Season the steak well, brush with a little oil and place on the upper rack on the halogen oven at 240C/475F.

3. Grill for 4-5 minutes each side or until the steak is cooked to your liking. Allow the steak to rest for a few minutes and then slice as thinly as possible.

4. Divide the meat and sautéed onion mixture across the sandwich rolls and place a cheese slice on top.

5. Close each sandwich roll over and individually wrap in foil. Turn down the halogen to 180C/350F and place the foil wrapped sandwiches on the lower rack to cook for 4-5 minutes.

BEEF STEW

Ingredients

- 700g stewing beef, cubed
- 1tbsp olive oil
- 3tbsp plain flour
- 4 slices bacon, chopped
- 1 onion, chopped
- 2 carrots, chopped
- 2 parsnips, chopped
- 4 garlic cloves, crushed
- 200g mushrooms, sliced
- 2tsp thyme
- 1tbsp Worcestershire sauce
- 120ml red wine
- 500ml beef stock
- Salt & pepper to season

Method

1. Brown the beef in a frying pan with the olive oil.

2. Remove the beef and place in a plastic bag with the plain flour and shake well to cover the meat.

3. Meanwhile gently sauté the bacon, onions, carrots, parsnips, garlic and mushrooms in the same frying pan for a few minutes.

4. Season well and add all the other ingredients to the pan. Stir well, bring to the boil and place in an ovenproof dish.

5. Cover tightly with foil, place on the lower rack and leave to cook in the halogen oven at 180C/350F for 60-70 minutes or until the beef is tender & cooked through.

6. Remove the lid for the last 10 minutes of cooking to reduce the liquid down if needed.

MOZZARELLA BAKED VEGGIES

SERVES 2

Ingredients

- 1tbsp olive oil
- 2 red peppers, sliced
- 2 garlic cloves, crushed
- 100g cherry tomatoes
- 100g baby corn
- 6 shallots
- 2 aubergines, sliced
- 100g pitted olives, halved
- 125g mozzarella cheese, chopped
- 2tbsp fresh basil, chopped
- Salt & pepper to season

Method

1. Combine all the ingredients, except the chopped basil, in an ovenproof dish.

2. Place on the lower rack and leave to cook in the halogen oven at 180C/350F for 40-50 minutes or until the vegetables are tender and cooked through.

RED CABBAGE CASSEROLE

SERVES 2

Ingredients

- 2 onions, chopped
- 2tsp fennel seeds
- 2tsp caraway seeds
- 1tbsp olive oil
- 1 large red cabbage, shredded
- 2tbsp horseradish sauce
- 2 apples, chopped
- 2tbsp butter
- Salt & pepper to season

Method

1. Gently sauté the onion, fennel & caraway seeds in the olive oil for a few minutes until softened.

2. Combine all the ingredients in an ovenproof dish, place on the lower rack, cover and leave to cook in the halogen oven at 200C/400F for 40-50 minutes or until the vegetables are tender and cooked through.

BAKED GARLIC MUSHROOMS

SERVES 2

Ingredients

- 1tbsp olive oil
- 4 garlic cloves, crushed
- 4 vine ripened tomatoes, chopped
- 100g Cheddar cheese, grated
- 125g Mozzarella cheese, chopped
- 1tbsp chopped chives
- 4 large portabella mushroom
- Cooking oil spray
- Salt & pepper to season

Method

1. Combine together the olive oil, garlic, tomatoes, cheeses & chives. Season well.

2. Put the mushrooms in an ovenproof dish, pile the tomato mix on top and place on the bottom rack of halogen oven.

3. Grill at 220C/425F for 10-12 minutes or until the mushrooms are tender and cooked through.

ROASTED PEPPER & GARLIC SALAD

SERVES 2

Ingredients

- 2tbsp balsamic vinegar
- 1tbsp olive oil
- 2 red onions, sliced
- 4 garlic cloves, crushed
- 2 red peppers, sliced
- 250g tomatoes, halved
- 200g mixed leaf salad
- 2tbsp fresh basil, chopped
- Salt & pepper to season

Method

1. Mix together the balsamic vinegar and oil with the onions, garlic, peppers and tomatoes.

2. Place in an ovenproof dish and cook in the halogen oven at 180C/350F for 20-30 minutes or until the vegetables are tender.

3. Season well and serve tossed through the salad leaves with the chopped basil sprinkled over the top. Pour any juices on the salad as a dressing.

SWEET & SOUR NOODLES

SERVES 4

Ingredients

- 2 garlic cloves, crushed
- 2 bags (640g) shredded vegetables & beansprouts
- 1 tin (230g) pineapple chunks
- 3tbsp soy sauce
- 1tsp brown sugar
- 1tbsp cider vinegar
- 2tbsp tomato purée
- 2tsp corn-flour
- 4tbsp water
- 200g egg noodles

Method

1. Add the garlic, vegetables, pineapple chunks (and juice form the tin) soy, sugar, vinegar and puree to an ovenproof dish.

2. Mix well, cover with foil and cook on the bottom rack of the halogen oven on 200C/400F for 10-20 minutes or until the vegetables are tender.

3. Meanwhile mix together the corn-flour and water to form a paste (use a little more water if needed).

4. Cook the noodles in salted boiling water until tender.

5. Once the vegetables are cooked stir through the corn-flour paste to thicken the sauce. Leave to cook for a minute or two longer and serve with the noodles.

MIXED BEAN CHILLI

Ingredients

- 3 onions, chopped
- 3 garlic cloves, crushed
- 2 carrots, diced
- 150g mushrooms, sliced
- 1tbsp olive oil
- 1 tin (400g) chopped tomatoes
- 2 tins (800g) mixed beans, drained
- 3tbsp tomato purée
- 1tsp each cumin, paprika & coriander
- 2tsp brown sugar
- 1tbsp fresh chives, chopped
- Salt & pepper to season

Method

1. Gently sauté the onion, garlic, carrots and mushroom in the olive oil for a few minutes until softened.
2. Combine all the ingredients, except the chopped chives, in an ovenproof dish.
3. Season well, cover with foil and place on the lower rack of the halogen oven. Leave to cook for 30-35 minutes at 200C/400F or until piping hot.
4. Sprinkle with chopped chives and serve.

ITALIAN BEANS

SERVES 2

Ingredients

- 350g Ditalini pasta
- 1 tin (400g) Borlotti beans, drained
- 2tsp rosemary
- 2 garlic cloves, crushed
- 3tbsp tomato purée
- 1 onion, chopped
- 60ml vegetable stock
- 2tbsp Parmesan cheese, grated
- Salt & pepper to season

Method

1. Cook the pasta in salted boiling water until tender.
2. Combine all the ingredients, except the Parmesan, in an ovenproof dish.
3. Place on the lower rack, cover and leave to cook in the halogen oven at 200C/400F for 20-25 minutes or until the pasta and beans are piping hot and cooked through.
4. Sprinkle over the cheese and serve.

DOUBLE CHEESE PIZZA

SERVES 2

Ingredients

- 1 packet yeast
- 250g plain flour
- 3tsp runny honey
- ½ salt
- 1tbsp extra virgin olive oil
- 200ml warm water
- 4tbsp tomato purée
- 2tsp garlic puree
- 4tbsp Parmesan cheese, grated
- 250g Mozzarella cheese, cubed
- 1 bunch fresh basil, chopped
- Cooking oil spray
- Salt & pepper to season

Method

1. Place the yeast, warm water and honey in a mixer. Slowly mix in the flour. Add the oil and salt and carefully mix. When the dough is formed take out of the mixer and bring together into one ball. Place back in the bowl and cover with cling film. Leave to rest for 30 minutes or until the dough has increased to double its original size.

2. Halve the dough in two and roll into two 25-30cm pizzas. It's best to roll out onto a piece of baking parchment to place on the tray.

3. Combine the tomato and garlic purées and spread onto the dough discs bases. Arrange the mozzarella over the top and spray with oil.

4. Cook at 200C/400F for 8-10 minutes, or until the bases are properly cooked and the topping is bubbling. Use both the upper and lower racks for the 2 pizza bases and swap half way through cooking.

5. Remove from the oven and sprinkle with fresh Parmesan and basil.

MACARONI CHEESE

SERVES 4

Ingredients

- 400g macaroni pasta
- 1tbsp Dijon mustard
- 250ml crème fraiche
- 60ml milk
- ½tsp nutmeg
- 300g Cheddar cheese, grated
- 100g spinach, chopped
- 8 vine ripened tomatoes, sliced
- Salt & pepper to season

Method

1. Cook the pasta in salted boiling water until tender.
2. Meanwhile gently warm through the mustard, crème fraiche, milk, nutmeg and cheese in a saucepan.
3. Combine all the ingredients in an ovenproof dish, laying the tomato slices on top.
4. Season well, cover and place on the lower rack of the halogen oven.
5. Leave to cook for 25-30 minutes at 200C/400F or until piping hot.

GREEN LENTIL & BEAN BAKE

SERVES 2

Ingredients

- 2 leeks, sliced
- 2 garlic cloves, crushed
- 1tbsp oil
- 2 courgettes, sliced
- 75g green beans, chopped
- 50g sundried tomatoes, chopped
- 1 tin (400g) green lentils, drained
- 120ml vegetable stock
- 1tbsp fresh flat leaf parsley, chopped
- Salt & pepper to season

Method

1. Gently sauté the leek and garlic in olive oil for a few minutes until softened.

2. Combine all the ingredients, except the chopped parsley, in an ovenproof dish. Place on the lower rack, and leave to cook in the halogen oven at 180C/350F for 30-40 minutes or until everything is tender and cooked through.

3. Sprinkle with parsely, season and serve.

HADDOCK & TOMATO STEW

SERVES 4

Ingredients

- 3 onions, chopped
- 3 garlic cloves, crushed
- 3tsp anchovy paste
- 1tbsp olive oil
- 400g small peeled prawns
- 300g boneless, skinless haddock fillets, cut into chunks
- 60ml fish stock
- 1 tin (400g) chopped tomatoes
- 1tbsp sundried tomato paste
- 1tbsp fresh basil, chopped
- 2 bay leaves
- Salt & pepper to season

Method

1. Gently sauté the onion, anchovy paste & garlic in the olive oil for a few minutes. Add all the ingredients to an ovenproof dish and season well.

2. Cover with foil, place on the lower rack and leave to cook in the halogen oven at 180C/350F for 30-35 minutes or until the seafood is properly cooked through.

CREAMY FISH & PRAWN BAKE

SERVES 4

Ingredients

- 3 slices brown bread
- 200ml milk
- 200g soft cream cheese
- 500g small peeled prawns
- 300g boneless white fish fillets, cut into chunks
- 200g spinach, chopped
- 2 lemons cut into wedges
- Salt & pepper to season

Method

1. Make the breadcrumbs by putting the bread and a pinch of salt & pepper into a food processor and pulse until you have breadcrumbs.

2. Gently heat the milk and cream cheese in a saucepan to make a creamy sauce. Carefully combine all the ingredients (except the lemon wedges) in an ovenproof dish, season and sprinkle the breadcrumbs on top.

3. Place on the lower rack and leave to cook in the halogen oven at 200C/400F for 25-35 minutes or until the seafood is properly cooked through and the vegetables are tender. Serve with lemon wedges on the side.

PRAWN & PEPPER KEBABS

SERVES 2

Ingredients

- 400g large king prawns
- 2tbsp olive oil
- 1tbsp lemon juice
- 1tsp each cumin, paprika & coriander
- 2 garlic cloves, crushed
- 1tsp brown sugar
- 2 baby gem lettuce, shredded
- 2 peppers, cut into pieces
- 3tsp mint sauce
- 4tbsp Greek yoghurt
- 4 metal kebab skewers
- 1 lemons cut into wedges
- Salt & pepper to season

Method

1. Mix together the oil, lemon juice, ground spices, garlic and sugar to form a paste. Season the prawns and pepper pieces and combine in the spice paste.

2. Place in a dish and leave for up to 1 hour to marinate.

3. Skewer the prawns and pepper pieces in turn to 4 kebabs. Place on the lower of the halogen oven on 240C/475F.

4. Grill for 3-5 minutes each side or until the prawns are cooked through and the pepper pieces are tender (take care handling the skewers as they will get hot).

5. Meanwhile mix the mint sauce and Greek yoghurt together.

6. Plate up the skewers along with the shredded lettuce and serve the lemon wedges and mint yoghurt on the side.

TUNA & NOODLE CASSEROLE

SERVES 4

Ingredients

- 3 onions, chopped
- 2tsp olive oil
- 3 tins tuna steak, drained
- 200g peas
- 400g fine egg noodles
- 1 tin (400g) chopped tomatoes
- 1tsp crushed chilli flakes
- 3tbsp sundried tomato paste
- 200g Cheddar cheese, grated
- Salt & pepper to season

Method

1. Gently sauté the onion in the olive oil for a few minutes until soft.
2. Meanwhile cook the noodles for a few minutes in salted boiling water until tender.
3. Combine all the ingredients really well in an ovenproof dish.
4. Season, place on the lower rack and leave to cook in the halogen oven at 200C/400F for 20-25 minutes or until piping hot.

GRILLED TUNA

SERVES 4

Ingredients

- 4 large boneless tuna steak
- 3tbsp balsamic vinegar
- 2tbsp soy sauce
- 2tbsp olive oil
- 1tbsp honey
- 2 bags (640g) beansprout & vegetable mix
- Salt & pepper to season

Method

1. Mix together the balsamic vinegar, soy sauce, oil and honey.

2. Place the tuna fillets on the lower rack of the halogen oven and brush with the balsamic/oil mix.

3. Cook for 6-10 minutes at 240C/475F or until the tuna is cooked to your preference (6 minutes of cooking will leave it quite rare).

4. Meanwhile use the rest of the balsamic/oil mix to stir-fry the beansprouts for a few minutes while the tuna cooks in the halogen oven. Add a little more soy sauce to the beansprouts during cooking if needed.

5. Serve the tuna steak on top of the stir-fried beansprouts and vegetables.

SWEET SOY SALMON

SERVES 4

Ingredients

- 2tbsp runny honey
- 2tbsp soy sauce
- 1tbsp sesame oil
- 4 thick skinless, boneless salmon fillets
- 400g asparagus spears
- 125g Gruyere cheese, grated
- 2 lemons cut into wedges
- Salt & pepper to season

Method

1. First mix together the honey, soy sauce and sesame oil.

2. Place the salmon fillets and asparagus in an ovenproof dish and combine with the honey soy mix.

3. Place on the lower rack of the halogen oven and cook for 8-12 minutes at 240C/475F or until the salmon fillets are properly cooked through and the asparagus spears are tender.

4. Sprinkle the cheese over the asparagus to melt for a few minutes before the end of cooking.

5. Serve with lemon wedges on the side.

SALMON PESTO FILLETS & SWEET POTATOES

SERVES 4

Ingredients

- 2 slices brown bread
- 2tbsp grated Parmesan cheese
- 3tbsp green pesto
- 4 thick skinless, boneless salmon fillets
- 800g sweet potato, peeled & cubed
- 200g mangetout
- Salt & pepper to season

Method

1. Make the breadcrumbs by putting the bread and a pinch of salt & pepper into a food processor and pulse until you have breadcrumbs.

2. Mix together the breadcrumbs, Parmesan & pesto and spread evenly over the top of the salmon fillets.

3. Place the salmon in an ovenproof dish on the lower rack of the halogen oven and cook for 10-15 minutes at 240C/475F or until the salmon is properly cooked through.

4. Meanwhile boil the sweet potato for 10 minutes or until tender.

5. Season well and mash a little with the back of a fork. Steam the mangetout for a few minutes on top of the boiling pan while the potatoes are cooking. Arrange the vegetables and fish together on a plate and serve.

LEMON SOLE GRATIN

SERVES 4

Ingredients

- 4 large boneless lemon sole fillets
- 200g mushrooms, chopped
- 4 garlic cloves, crushed
- 2 onions, chopped
- 1tbsp anchovy paste
- 1tbsp olive oil
- 4 slices brown bread
- 2tbsp grated Parmesan cheese
- 4tbsp fresh flat leaf parsley, chopped
- 8 tomatoes
- 200g rocket leaves
- 2 lemons cut into wedges
- Salt & pepper to season

Method

1. Slice each lemon sole fillet to create a cavity for stuffing.

2. Gently sauté the mushrooms, garlic, onions & anchovy paste together in a little olive oil for a few minutes. Stuff this mixture equally into each fillet.

3. Make the breadcrumbs by putting the bread and a pinch of salt & pepper into a food processor and pulse until you have breadcrumbs.

4. Mix together the breadcrumbs, Parmesan and chopped parsley.

5. Place the stuffed fillet and tomatoes in an ovenproof dosh on the lower rack of the halogen oven. Season and sprinkle with the breadcrumb mix.

6. Cook for 8-12 minutes at 240C/475F or until the fish is properly cooked through. Serve with the rocket salad and lemon wedges.

SALMON FISH PIE

SERVES 4

Ingredients

- 600g boneless salmon fillets
- 2 carrots, finely chopped
- 400ml milk
- 800g potatoes, peeled and cubed
- 100g peas
- 100g sweetcorn
- 2tbsp butter
- 1tbsp plain flour
- 2tsp Dijon mustard
- 200g Cheddar cheese, grated
- Salt & pepper to season

Method

1. Place the fish and carrots in a pan and cover with milk. Poach for 8-10 minutes until the fish is cooked and flakes easily with a fork.

2. Remove the fish from the pan and reserve the milk.

3. Place the cooked fish, sweetcorn, carrots & peas in an ovenproof dish.

4. Meanwhile, cook the potatoes in salted boiling water until tender. When they are ready, drain and mash using a splash of the fishy milk and a little butter.

5. Gently melt the rest of the butter in a pan and stir through the flour. When you have made a roux (paste) begin adding the reserved fishy milk and continue stirring. The sauce will thicken after a minute or two.

6. Add the mustard and cheese and pour onto the fish and vegetables in the ovenproof dish.

7. Cover with the smooth mash, place on the lower rack of the halogen oven and cook at 200C/400F for 20-30 minutes until browned and piping hot.

HOMEMADE FISH FINGERS

SERVES 4

Ingredients

- 600g firm boneless white fish fillets
- 4 slices brown bread
- 1tsp oregano
- 1tsp paprika
- 3 free range eggs
- 3tbsp plain flour
- 2 lemons
- Cooking oil spray
- Mayonnaise & ketchup to serve
- Salt & pepper to season

Method

1. First slice the fish fillets into thick strips.

2. Make the breadcrumbs by putting the bread and a pinch of salt & pepper into a food processor and pulse until you have breadcrumbs.

3. Sieve the flour onto a plate and combine with the paprika and oregano.

4. Put the breadcrumbs on a separate plate and beat the eggs in a bowl.

5. Cover each fish strip with flour by rolling them on the flour plate and then dip each strip in the egg. Finally coat well in the breadcrumbs.

6. Spray with cooking oil and place on a grill pan at the bottom of the halogen oven on 200C/400F for 8-12 minutes or until the fish is cooked through and the breadcrumbs are golden brown – increase the temperature if necessary.

7. Cut the lemon into wedges and serve the fish fingers with mayo and ketchup.

SULTANA SARDINES

SERVES 2

Ingredients

- 2 slices bread
- 3 garlic cloves, crushed
- 1 onion, chopped
- 4tbsp sultanas, chopped
- 1tbsp olive oil
- 8 whole fresh sardines, gutted and cleaned
- 1tbsp fresh flat leaf parsley, chopped
- 2 lemons cut into wedges
- Salt & pepper to serve

Method

1. Make the breadcrumbs by putting the bread and a pinch of salt & pepper into a food processor and pulse until you have breadcrumbs.
2. Gently sauté the garlic, onions & sultanas in the olive oil for a few minutes until softened, then combine with the breadcrumbs.
3. Place the sardines on a baking tray, brush with a little olive oil and stuff the sultana mix into the gutted sardines.
4. Season well, place on the bottom rack of the halogen over and cook for 8-12 minutes at 240C/475F or until the sardines are properly cooked through. Serve with lemon wedges at the side.

POLLACK & PEANUT BUTTER

SERVES 4

Ingredients

- 4 boneless, white fish fillets
- 2tbsp peanut butter
- 3tbsp soy sauce
- 6 large vine ripened tomatoes, sliced
- 2 red onions sliced into rounds
- 1 tin (400g) tinned kidney beans, drained
- Salad dressing to serve
- Salt & pepper to season

Method

1. Mix together the peanut butter paste and soy sauce.

2. Put the fillets in an ovenproof dish, spread the peanut butter on top and cover with foil.

3. Place on the bottom rack of the halogen oven and cook for 10-15 minutes at 240C/475F or until the fish is properly cooked through.

4. Meanwhile arrange the kidney beans, sliced tomatoes and onion slices on a plate. Season and serve with a little salad dressing and the cooked fish.

ROASTED VEG

Ingredients

- 200g new potatoes, quartered
- 2 red peppers, halved
- 2 red onions, cut into wedges
- 12 cherry tomatoes
- 1tsp paprika
- 1tsp mixed dried herbs
- 2tbsp olive oil
- 1tsp crushed sea salt
- Salt & pepper to season

Method

1. Place all ingredients into a bowl and combine well until everything is properly coated in oil.

2. Spread out onto on a baking tray on the lower rack of the halogen oven and cook at 200C/400F for 20-30minutes or until tender (move to up to the upper shelf and increase the heat to brown if needed) .

CHILLI POTATO WEDGES

Ingredients

- 500g potatoes
- 2tbsp olive oil
- 2tsp crushed sea salt
- 2 garlic cloves, crushed
- 1tsp chilli flakes
- Salt & pepper to season

Method

1. Leave the potatoes unpeeled and cut into wedges. In a bowl combine together the wedges, oil, salt, garlic and chilli flakes.

2. Place on a baking tray in a single layer on the lower rack and leave to cook in the halogen oven at 220C/450F for 25-35 minutes or until golden & tender.

TURMERIC RICE

SERVES 4

Ingredients

- 2 onions, chopped
- 1tbsp olive oil
- 400g Basmati rice
- 750ml cups vegetable stock
- 2 bay leaves
- 1tbsp turmeric
- 100g sweetcorn
- 100g peas
- Salt & pepper to season

Method

1. Gently sauté the onion in the olive oil for a few minutes. Add all the ingredients to the pan and bring to the boil.

2. Transfer to an ovenproof dish and cover with foil.

3. Place on the lower rack and leave to cook in the halogen oven at 200C/400F for 25-35 minutes or until the rice is tender. Add a little more stock if needed. Remove the bay leaves, drain, season and serve.

ASPARAGUS & PARMESAN

Ingredients

- 1tbsp olive oil
- 400g asparagus
- 2 garlic cloves, crushed
- 3tbsp Parmesan cheese, grated
- Salt & pepper to season

Method

1. Combine all the ingredients and place in an ovenproof dish.
2. Season well, place on the high rack of the halogen oven and cook at 240C/475F for 6-10 minutes or until tender.

CAULIFLOWER CHEESE

SERVES 4

Ingredients

- 2 slices brown bread
- 2 cauliflowers, broken into florets
- 2 onions, chopped
- 150g soft cream cheese
- 60ml milk
- Salt & pepper to season

Method

1. Make the breadcrumbs by putting the bread and a pinch of salt & pepper into a food processor and pulse until you have breadcrumbs.

2. Steam the cauliflower florets until tender. Meanwhile gently heat together the cream cheese, onions and milk.

3. Place the cauliflower in an ovenproof dish and pour over the cream cheese sauce. Season well and sprinkle over the breadcrumbs.

4. Place on the lower rack and leave to cook in the halogen oven at 240C/475F for 5-10 minutes or until golden brown.

BAKED POTATOES

SERVES 2

Ingredients

- 2 large baking potatoes
- 1tbsp olive oil
- 2tsp crushed sea salt
- 1tbsp butter
- 200ml soured cream
- Salt & pepper to season

Method

1. Pierce the potatoes with a fork and use your hands to rub in the oil and crushed salt.

2. Place on the lower grill rack of the halogen oven and cook at 200C/400F for 50-60 minutes or until tender. Cut in half, season well, place the butter inside to melt.

3. Add a dollop of soured cream and serve.

ROSEMARY & GARLIC MUSHROOMS

SERVES 4

Ingredients

- 2tbsp olive oil
- 600g chestnut mushrooms, sliced
- 2 garlic cloves, crushed
- 2tbsp fresh rosemary, chopped
- Salt & pepper to season

Method

1. Place all the ingredients in an ovenproof dish.

2. Season well, place on the high rack of the halogen oven and cook at 240C/475F for 6-10 minutes or until tender.

SWEET POTATO FRIES

Ingredients

- 500g sweet potatoes
- 1tsp paprika
- 1tbsp olive oil
- 2tsp brown sugar
- 1tsp crushed sea salt

Method

1. Cut the potatoes into thin slices and then in rows to make thin French fries, keeping them all a similar size.
2. Put the raw fries into a bowl and coat with paprika, olive oil, salt and sugar. Mix really well to make sure they are properly covered.
3. Spread out onto on a baking tray on the lower rack of the halogen oven and cook at 200C/400F for 10-15 or until tender and crispy (move to up to the upper shelf and increase the heat to brown the fries if needed).

GRILLED TOMATOES & AUBERGINES

SERVES 2

Ingredients

- 6 tomatoes, thinly sliced
- 2 aubergines, thinly sliced
- 3tbsp olive oil
- 2 garlic cloves, crushed
- 3tbsp fresh sage, chopped
- Salt & pepper to season

Method

1. In a bowl combine together the tomatoes, aubergine, oil and garlic,
2. Lay the tomatoes and aubergine in a single layer in an ovenproof dish and place on the upper rack of the halogen oven. Cook for 10-15 minutes at 240C/475F or until browned and tender.
3. Sprinkle the fresh sage over for the last few minutes of cooking.

BAKED SWEET POTATO

SERVES 2

Ingredients

- 1-2tbsp olive oil
- 4tsp crushed sea salt
- 4 large sweet potatoes
- 6 garlic cloves, unpeeled
- 2tbsp butter
- Salt & pepper to season

Method

1. Pierce the potatoes with a fork and use your hands to rub the oil and crushed salt into the skins of the potatoes and garlic cloves

2. Place on a baking tray on the lower grill rack and leave to cook in the halogen oven at 200C/400F for 50-60 minutes or until tender.

3. Cut the potatoes in half and scoop out the flesh. Squeeze the garlic cloves out of their skins and mash with a fork together.

4. Mix the garlic and soft potato flesh together, season and serve with the butter melting on top.

LEMONY GREENS

Ingredients

- 2 pak choi
- 200g shredded spring greens
- 2tbsp olive oil
- 1tsp crushed sea salt
- 1 lemon
- Salt & pepper to season

Method

1. Split each pak choi in half.
2. Place all ingredients, except the lemon, into a bowl and combine well until everything is properly coated in oil.
3. Spread out onto on a baking tray on the lower rack of the halogen oven and cook at 200C/400F for 20-30 minutes or until tender (move to up to the upper shelf and increase the heat to brown if needed).
4. Serve with a wedge of lemon.

BAKED BEETROOT

SERVES 4

Ingredients

- 800g fresh beetroot
- 2tbsp olive oil
- 2tbsp balsamic vinegar
- 50g pine nuts
- Salt & pepper to season

Method

1. Place all ingredients into a bowl and combine well until everything is properly coated in oil.

2. Spread out onto on a baking tray on the lower rack of the halogen oven, cover with foil and cook at 200C/400F for 20-30 minutes or until tender.

3. Remove the foil and cook for a few minutes longer if needed.

ROOT VEG GRATIN

Ingredients

- 400g celeriac, sliced
- 200g potatoes, sliced
- 200g swede, sliced
- 4 carrots, sliced
- 1tsp mixed dried herbs
- 2tbsp butter, melted
- 1tsp crushed sea salt
- Salt & pepper to season

Method

1. Place all ingredients into a bowl and combine well until everything is properly coated in oil.

2. Spread out onto on a baking tray on the lower rack of the halogen oven and cook at 200C/400F for 40-60minutes or until tender (move to up to the upper shelf and increase the heat to brown if needed).

PEPPERONI PITTA SNACK

SERVES 2

Ingredients

- 2 large pitta bread
- 4tbsp tomato purée
- 6 tomatoes, chopped
- 1 onion, sliced
- 250g Cheddar cheese, grated
- 100g pepperoni slices
- 2tbsp fresh basil, chopped
- Cooking oil spray
- Salt & pepper to season

Method

1. Slice the pitta breads lengthways in half to make 4 pitta pizza bases. Spread the tomato purée over each pitta base. Arrange the tomatoes, onion, cheese and pepperoni slices on the top.

2. Spray with a little cooking oil spray and place on the top grill rack of the halogen oven at 220C/425F and cook for 6-10 minutes or until the pizzas are cooked through.

MARMITE CHEESE ON TOAST

SERVES 4

Ingredients

- 4 slices thick seeded bread
- 1tsp butter
- 1tbsp Marmite
- 200g Cheddar cheese, grated
- 100g Red Leicester cheese, grated
- Salt & pepper to season

Method

1. Gently spread the butter and marmite over the bread slices.
2. Sprinkle with the two cheeses, season and place on the top grill rack of the halogen oven.
3. Cook at 240C/475F for 4-5 minutes or until brown and bubbling.

TOMATO & CHEESE CIABATTA

Ingredients

- 2tbsp sundried tomato purée
- 2 ciabatta rolls
- 200g Cheddar cheese, grated
- 4 large tomatoes, sliced
- 2tbsp fresh basil leaves, chopped
- Salt & pepper to season

Method

1. Halve the ciabatta rolls and spread with tomato purée.

2. Lay the sliced tomatoes on top and cover with cheese.

3. Season and place on the top grill rack of the halogen oven to cook at cook at 240C/475F for 4-5 minutes or until the cheese is melted.

4. Sprinkle with chopped basil and serve.

RAREBIT MUFFIN

Ingredients

- 2 breakfast muffins
- 1tbsp butter
- 1tbsp plain flour
- 60ml cup milk
- 200g Cheddar cheese, grated
- 4 free range eggs
- 2tsp Dijon mustard
- Salt & pepper to season

Method

1. Halve the muffins and place on a baking tray.

2. Heat the butter in a pan and stir in the flour. Add the milk and quickly whisk until smooth.

3. Take off the heat and mix in the cheese, eggs and mustard. Pile on top of the breakfast muffins halves, season and place on the top grill rack of the halogen oven.

4. Cook at 240C/475F for 4-5 minutes or until brown and bubbling.

PARMA HAM PANINI

Ingredients

- 2 paninis, sliced
- 4 slices Gouda cheese
- 4 slices Parma ham
- 2 large tomatoes, sliced
- Salt & pepper to season

Method

1. Halve the Panini rolls and lay the ham on top.

2. Add the sliced tomatoes and cover with cheese.

3. Season and place on the top grill rack of the halogen oven to cook at 240C/475F for 4-5 minutes or until brown and bubbling.

GARLIC BREAD FINGERS

SERVES 4

Ingredients

- 1 ciabatta loaf
- 2tbsp butter
- 1tbsp olive oil
- 6 garlic cloves, crushed
- Salt & pepper to season

Method

1. Split the loaf in half and cut into ciabatta batons about 2cm wide.
2. Place all ingredients into a bowl and combine well until everything is properly coated in oil.
3. Spread out onto on a baking tray on the upper rack of the halogen oven and cook at 200C/400F for 6-10 minutes or crispy.

TAPENADE BITES

Ingredients

- 2 paninis
- 4tbsp tomato purée
- 12 pitted black olives, finely chopped
- 6 sundried tomatoes, finely chopped
- 1tbsp olive oil
- Salt & pepper to season

Method

1. Combine together the puree, olives and sundried tomatoes to make a simple tapenade.

2. Split the paninis in half and cut into bite size cubes about 4cm wide.

3. Place all ingredients into a bowl and combine well until everything is properly coated in the tapenade.

4. Spread out onto on a baking tray on the upper rack of the halogen oven and cook at 200C/400F for 4-6 minutes or crispy.

SPICED NUTS

Ingredients

- 400g mixed nuts
- 1tbsp curry powder
- 2tbsp brown sugar
- ½tsp ginger
- 1tsp sea salt flakes
- 2tbsp olive oil

Method

1. Place all ingredients into a bowl and combine well until everything is properly coated in oil.

2. Spread out onto on a baking tray on the upper rack of the halogen oven and cook at 200C/400F for 6-10 minutes.

3. When the nuts are golden and caramelized serve with a little more salt if you wish.

CHEESY PINWHEELS

SERVES 4

Ingredients

- 200g Cheddar cheese, grated
- 3tbsp Branston pickle
- 1tbsp Dijon mustard
- 1tbsp plain flour
- 1 readymade roll (320g) puff pastry
- 1 egg
- Salt & pepper to season

Method

1. Combine together the cheese, pickle and mustard.

2. Dust the flour onto the worktop and lay the pastry on top.

3. Spread the cheese and pickle mix over the pastry, roll up into a sausage and cut into 12 slices to make the pinwheels.

4. Lay the slices on a greased baking tray. Beat the egg and brush over the pinwheels.

5. Place on the lower rack of the halogen oven and cook at 200C/400F for 10-15 minutes or until golden and cooked through.

BLACKBERRY CRUMBLE

SERVES 4

Ingredients

- 600g ripe blackberries
- 3tbsp sugar
- 2tbsp water
- 1tbsp golden syrup
- 300g oats
- 100g butter, melted
- 200ml single cream

Method

1. Mix together the sugar, water and blackberries.

2. Put in an ovenproof dish place on the lower rack and cook in the halogen oven for 8-10 minutes at 200C/400F.

3. Meanwhile mix together the syrup, oats & melted butter and spread on top of the blackberries.

4. Return to the oven and cook for a further 14-18 minutes.

5. Serve with the cream poured over the top.

BAKED PEACHES

Ingredients

- 2 tins (800g) sliced peaches
- 1tbsp brown sugar
- 1tsp vanilla extract
- 400ml Greek yoghurt
- 1tbsp honey
- 1tsp nutmeg

Method

1. Mix together the sugar, vanilla extract and peach slices.

2. Place in an ovenproof dish on the lower rack of the halogen oven and cook for 10-12 minutes at 200C/400F.

3. Dollop the yoghurt on top, drizzle the honey over and add a pinch of nutmeg.

PEAR PUDDING

Ingredients

- 2tbsp honey
- 2tbsp orange juice
- 4 ripe pears, peeled, cored and halved
- 2tbsp Greek yoghurt
- 1tsp nutmeg

Method

1. Mix together the honey and orange juice.

2. Place the pear halves in an ovenproof dish and brush all over with the honey and juice.

3. Cover with foil place on the lower rack and leave to cook in the halogen oven for 20-25 minutes at 180C/350F or until the pears are tender.

4. Serve with Greek yoghurt on the side sprinkled with a pinch of ground nutmeg.

STICKY GOLDEN SYRUP PUDDING

SERVES 2

Ingredients

- 125g butter
- 125g brown sugar
- 125g self raising flour, sieved
- 3 free range eggs
- 1tsp olive oil
- 4tbsp golden syrup

Method

1. Cream together the butter and sugar before adding the eggs and flour until the pudding mixture is smooth.

2. Use the olive oil to grease a small ovenproof dish.

3. Add the syrup to the bottom of the dish and pour the pudding mixture on top.

4. Place on the lower rack of the halogen oven and cook for 20-25 minutes at 220C/425F or until the pudding has risen and is cooked through.

5. Tip the pudding out to serve.

BAKED APPLE & SULTANAS

SERVES 4

Ingredients

- 4 large cooking apples
- 3tbsp runny honey
- 2tsp brown sugar
- 2tbsp warm water
- 4tbsp sultanas
- 1tsp each nutmeg & cinnamon
- 4tbsp crème fraiche

Method

1. Leave the apples peeled and core to create a cavity.

2. Mix together the honey, sugar, water, sultanas and spices.

3. Stuff the cored apples with the mixture and place in an ovenproof dish.

4. Place on the lower rack and cook in the halogen oven for 20-30 minutes at 200C/400F or until the apples are tender.

5. Serve with crème fraiche dolloped on top of each apple.

HONEY BANANAS & YOGHURT

SERVES 2

Ingredients

- 4 bananas, sliced
- 2tbsp runny honey
- 2tbsp Greek yoghurt
- Pinch of cinnamon

Method

1. Place the bananas in an ovenproof dish and combine with the honey and cinnamon.
2. Cover with foil and place on the lower rack to cook in the halogen oven for 10-15 minutes at 220C/450F.
3. Serve with the Greek yoghurt dolloped on top.

Printed in Great Britain
by Amazon